❦ History *of* Britain ❦
Shakespeare and the Theatre

Andrew Langley

Illustrated by John James

HISTORY OF BRITAIN – SHAKESPEARE AND THE THEATRE
was produced for Heinemann Children's Reference
by Lionheart Books, London

First published in Great Britain by Heinemann
Children's Reference, an imprint of Heinemann
Educational Publishers, a division of Reed
Educational and Professional Publishing Limited,
Halley Court, Jordan Hill, Oxford OX2 8EJ

MADRID ATHENS
FLORENCE PRAGUE WARSAW
PORTSMOUTH NH CHICAGO SAO PAULO MEXICO
SINGAPORE TOKYO MELBOURNE AUCKLAND
IBADAN GABORONE JOHANNESBURG KAMPALA NAIROBI

Editors: Lionel Bender, Sue Reid
Designer: Ben White
Editorial Assistant: Madeleine Samuel
Picture Researcher: Jennie Karrach
Media Conversion: Peter MacDonald
Typesetting: R & B Partnership

Educational Consultant: Jane Shuter
Editorial Advisors: Andrew Farrow, Paul Shuter

Production Controller: David Lawrence
Editorial Director: David Riley

ISBN 0 600 58834 3 Hb
ISBN 0 600 58835 1 Pb

British Library Cataloguing-in-Publication Data.
A catalogue record for this book is available from
the British Library.

Printed in Italy

Acknowledgements
Picture Credits FI = Fotomas Index, NPG = National Portrait Gallery,
London, BAL = Bridgeman Art Library. RHPL = Robert Harding Picture
Library.
t = top, b = bottom, l = left, r = right, c = centre.
Page 4bl: By kind permission of the Vicar and Churchwardens of Holy
Trinity Church, Stratford-upon-Avon/The Shakespeare Birthplace Trust,
Stratford-upon-Avon. 4c: FI. 5t: FI. 6l: RHPL. 6r: British Library/
Additional 18991, 924.651. 7: NPG 5175. 8l: e.t. archive. 9t: NPG
No.1. 9br: FI. 9bl: Lionheart Books. 10tr: NPG 2752. 10c: The Parker
Library/Corpus Christi College, Cambridge. 10b: British Library/maps
162.0.1. det 9540177. 12b: FI. 13t: By courtesy of the Duke of
Buccleuch and Queensbury KT. 13b: FI. 14b: FI. 15t: FI. 15b: FI. 16c:
Public Record Office, C66/1608. 16b: Christie's Colour Library. 17t:
BAL/Dulwich Picture Gallery, London 68313. 17bl: The Mansell
Collection. 18t: NPG. 18-19: British Library/Harley 7368 folio 9. 19tl:
Shakespeare Birthplace Trust. 19tr: FI. 20: FI. 21tl: FI. 21tr:
Woodmansterne Publications Ltd. 21bl: Public Record Office/Prob
1.4. 22tr: RHPL/Roy Rainford. 22br: RHPL/Adam Wolfitt. 22bl: British
Council/Mark Hakansson.

All artwork by John James except map page 23, by Hayward Art
Group.

Cover: Artwork by John James. Photos – manuscript (Public Record
Office); painting of players (British Library); sketch of the Globe (e.t.
archive); Catalogue (Shakespeare Birthplace Trust).

PLACES TO VISIT

Here are some museums and sites where you can find out
more about William Shakespeare. Your local tourist office will
be able to tell you about other interesting places to visit in
your area.

In or near Stratford-upon-Avon:
Anne Hathaway's Cottage, Shottery. The farmhouse, very
near the town, where Shakespeare's wife grew up.
Holy Trinity Church Contains Shakespeare's grave and his
memorial.
The Knot Garden A re-creation of the famous garden of
intertwining hedges laid out by Shakespeare at New Place.
Mary Arden's House, Wilmcote. The family home of the
poet's mother, beautifully preserved and containing
fascinating period implements.
Royal Shakespeare Theatre Home of the Royal
Shakespeare Company, and the very best place to see
performances of his plays.
Shakespeare's Birthplace One of the country's most
famous tourist spots: it can be very crowded!

Outside Stratford:
The Globe Theatre, Bankside, London. A faithful
reconstruction of the Globe of 1614, in much the same
materials. Performances began in 1995.
Museum of London The exhibition includes many items from
the London of Shakespeare's time.

INTRODUCTION

William Shakespeare is the most famous writer in history. His plays are still published, read and performed all over the world. His words and phrases are used by ordinary people every day. His ideas about greed, hate, power, love, death and many other things still influence the way we think.

Yet Shakespeare lived and worked 400 years ago, during the reigns of Elizabeth I and James I. Although his plays give a vivid picture of this period, little is known about the sort of man he was, or about his private life. The only evidence, apart from the plays and poems, comes from official documents, such as church registers, tax records and wills. From these we can build up a picture of his life and times.

CONTENTS

STRATFORD BOY

William Shakespeare was born in Stratford-upon-Avon around 23 April 1564. He died in Stratford 52 years later. Although he became successful and famous, he never forgot his birthplace. It was a busy market town which lay on an important trade route between the Midlands and the port of Bristol.

▽ **Shakespeare's birthplace in Stratford-upon-Avon**, Warwickshire, as it looked in 1769. It was already attracting tourists. The house can still be visited today.

▽ **William Shakespeare's baptism** is recorded in the register of Holy Trinity Church, Stratford. The Latin entry means, "William, son of John Shakespeare". This is the first written reference to the poet. The date is 26 April 1564.

William was the third of eight children. His father, John, was a glovemaker. His workshop was in part of the large family house in the centre of Stratford. John Shakespeare became an important figure in the town, and was made bailiff, or mayor, of Stratford in 1568.

William's mother, Mary, came from a rich farming family in a nearby village. Her wealth helped John Shakespeare build up his business. Mary was a calm and intelligent woman, who gave her children a comfortable and happy upbringing.

At the age of seven, William probably started at the local grammar school. He later described the typical schoolboy, "with shining morning face, creeping like snail unwillingly to school". The school day was long, beginning at 6 a.m., and the work was hard. The main subjects were Latin and English. The pupils had to learn long passages by heart, and any mistakes were punished with a beating.

◁ **Young William Shakespeare and a friend in the crowded Stratford streets**, where there were many excitements to be seen.

△ **A typical Tudor schoolroom.** The master sits with his cane near to hand. The artist shows the pupils as tiny adults, not as children.

In his spare time, William must have explored the countryside around the town. To the north was the mysterious Forest of Arden (which he was to use as the setting for *As You Like It*). To the south were open fields, where "daisies pied and violets blue...do paint the meadows with delight". His poems and plays show that he knew a lot about flowers and animals.

When William was 13, disaster struck the family. John got into debt and lost his position as town official. Soon afterwards, William probably left school, perhaps to work for his father and earn much-needed money. But we know nothing definite until 1582, when he got married. His bride was Anne Hathaway, a farmer's daughter. She was eight years older than William – and already pregnant with their first child.

WANDERING ACTOR

William and Anne Shakespeare's first child, Susanna, was born in 1583. Two years later they had twins, called Hamnet and Judith. The baptisms of all three children are recorded in the church register. They were all still living at John Shakespeare's house. William would have looked for work to support his growing family, and for a chance to break away.

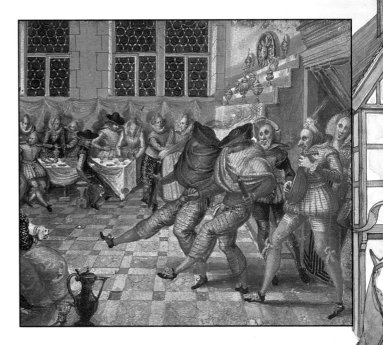

▽ **Travelling players** in bright costumes and with musical instruments entertain nobles at a private performance – from a painting of 1610.

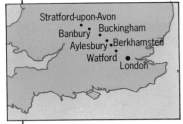

◁ **A map of southern England in about 1587**, showing the route that Shakespeare may have taken from Stratford to London with a company of actors. The journey would have taken three or four days by horse-drawn wagon.

◁ **Anne Hathaway's Cottage, in Shottery near Stratford.** It is a large farmhouse which had belonged to Anne's father, Richard Hathaway, who died in 1581.

It was probably at this time that Shakespeare had his first taste of acting. He had already seen short plays, dances and costume parades put on in Stratford by local people. Troupes of travelling players (actors) from London also made regular summer tours, performing in the streets and inn yards of the town.

Shakespeare was so thrilled by them that he decided to become an actor himself. This meant that he would have to leave Stratford and move to London, which was the centre of theatrical life. But at least he would be earning money.

In Elizabethan times, play-going was a favourite pastime. People enjoyed plays as much as we enjoy television today. Besides the acting companies of London, there were groups of actors supported by rich noblemen, and even by Queen Elizabeth herself. The 'Queen's Men' performed in Stratford in 1586.

Shakespeare may have got to know some of these players and persuaded them to give him work, probably doing odd carpentry jobs and playing small roles. Some time before 1587 he made the important move to London.

London in 1587 was an overcrowded, smelly and exciting city. With 200,000 inhabitants, it must have seemed a huge place to Shakespeare.

London was an important centre of trade, to which ships brought exotic cargoes from all over the world. Queen Elizabeth and her court lived in the city, and writers, artists and musicians came, like Shakespeare, to seek their fortunes.

◁ **England's ruler, Elizabeth I**, at her coronation in 1559.

▷ **Shakespeare and fellow actors' first glimpse of London.** The busy life of the city, with courtiers, foreign merchants, beggars and thieves, gave him much material for his plays.

△ **London was already a magnificent city.** The great London Bridge crossed the River Thames. On it can be seen shops, houses, and even a prison.

THE WOODEN O

The 1570s had marked the start of a great age in English drama. Two of the first theatres, The Theatre and The Curtain, were built in London. Before this, plays had been performed in courtyards or public halls, or in private theatres owned by wealthy men.

▽ **A view of the Globe during a performance.** The theatre was circular but with many sides, and made of timber and thatch. It burned to the ground in 1613. A new Globe was built on the same site in 1614.

▽ **The original Globe Theatre** was built in Southwark, south London in 1599. Shakespeare's company acted here.

The new Globe Theatre was built around a courtyard or pit. Here stood the poorer spectators (called the groundlings) open to the weather and the hands of pick-pockets. Those who paid more could sit under cover in one of the three levels of galleries. Altogether, The Globe could hold about 2,500 people – far more than most modern theatres.

The stage was a large platform which jutted out into the pit. The groundlings crowded right up to the stage and some even leaned on it during performances. The actors entered through two doors at the back. Behind these were the dressing rooms. A roof covered the stage area.

There was no painted scenery, but the plays were made more exciting by special effects. The stage had a trap door, through which actors could appear or disappear. Above the stage was an upper platform, which could be used as a balcony or a castle wall. Above this was another room, where the sound and lighting effects were made.

△ **A portrait by an unknown artist** of "Shakespeare, William, dramatist and poet".

▷ **This drawing of the Swan Theatre in Bankside, London**, was copied from a sketch made by a Dutch visitor, Johannes de Witt, in 1596. It is the only picture from the time to show what the inside of an Elizabethan theatre looked like.

△ **Some Elizabethan London theatres**, including The Globe, are shown on these stamps.

Between 1576 and 1614 nine new theatres were built in London. They could not be built inside the city walls because the councillors thought plays encouraged bad behaviour. These new theatres greatly benefitted their owners. When plays were performed in the streets, spectators only paid when a hat was passed round. In specially built theatres, they had to pay before going in.

THE PLAYERS

Shakespeare often mentioned actors in his plays. "Life's but a walking shadow, " he wrote in *Macbeth*, "a poor player that struts and frets his hour upon the stage, and then is heard no more." But it was only during his lifetime that they became respectable. Earlier, actors had been scorned as tramps or beggars.

In 1572, a law was passed making it illegal for anyone to perform without a licence. This forced actors to form permanent companies, and to find a nobleman to be their patron (protector). They became his servants, and named their company after him.

The actors had to raise money to keep the company going. Anyone who put money into an acting company was called a 'sharer', and shared in the profits. But there were also many expenses. Actors had to buy costumes, licences and equipment, and hire musicians and door-keepers. The owner of the theatre demanded a large fee.

▷ **Ben Jonson**, a friend of Shakespeare and a successful playwright.

▷ **Christopher Marlowe (1564-1593)** was a brilliant playwright who must have inspired Shakespeare. He died in a tavern brawl.

▷ **(Below) A detailed view of London**, drawn in Shakespeare's lifetime by Claes Visscher. It shows a stretch of the Thames, with St. Paul's Church and the city on the north bank. On the south bank are two theatres, The Bear Garden (also called The Hope), and The Globe. Visscher has drawn The Globe as a many-sided building, not a perfectly round one. This was the original Globe.

Shakespeare was probably part of a company of eight or more sharers, with several more hired actors. These included boys, who took all the female roles (women were not allowed to act until 1662). The actors had to work very hard. They performed six days a week, and in one season might act in more than 30 different plays.

Clearly, each company needed a regular supply of new plays. This must have encouraged Shakespeare to become a playwright. He probably began to write in the late 1580s, for his earliest plays, such as *Titus Andronicus* and *Henry VI*, were first performed in 1590. They were hugely successful, and Shakespeare's fame grew rapidly.

◁ **Bustle behind the scenes in the 'tiring house' (dressing room) at The Globe Theatre** as the actors get ready for a performance. Can you see:
● the audience through the stage door
● the leading actor about to go on stage
● the playwright checking the actors know their lines
● one actor helping another to put on his woman's gown
● the special effects man climbing into the upper floor
● the trumpet and drum used for fanfares
● the lute used to accompany songs
● the swords, ready for a battle scene?

PLAGUE AND POETRY

In 1592, the writer Robert Greene wrote of "an upstart crow that supposes he is as well able to bombast out a blank verse (write a simple poem) as the rest of you", who was "the only Shake-scene in a country". This shows that Shakespeare was making his rivals jealous.

By this time, Shakespeare had written five or six plays, including *Richard III* and *The Comedy of Errors*. But now his stage career came to a sudden halt. The plague (a deadly disease) broke out in London. It spread rapidly in the dirty streets and killed over 20,000 people.

London's councillors ordered that all theatres should be closed during the outbreak. The actors' companies were forced to leave the capital and take their plays on tour. Some companies went north, some went west, while others travelled as far as Holland and Germany.

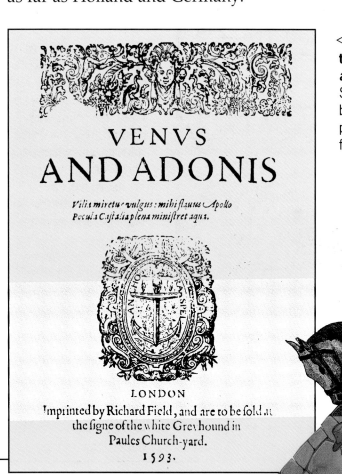

VENVS

AND ADONIS

Vilia miretur vulgus : mihi flauus Apollo
Pocula Castalia plena ministret aqua.

LONDON

Imprinted by Richard Field, and are to be sold at
the signe of the white Greyhound in
Paules Church-yard.
1593.

◁ **The title page of the long poem *Venus and Adonis***, the first of Shakespeare's works to be published. It was printed by a neighbour from Stratford.

While the theatres were closed, Shakespeare probably returned to Stratford to see his wife and children and get on with his writing. But he was not composing plays. Instead, he completed two long poems – *Venus and Adonis*, and *The Rape of Lucrece* which retold stories of love and violence by the Latin poet Ovid. These were the only works published by Shakespeare himself.

Shakespeare turned to poetry because the Elizabethans rated it more highly than drama. Besides, Shakespeare's plays did not belong to him: they were the property of his actors' company. But poetry might win him lasting fame.

Shakespeare dedicated both poems to the young Earl of Southampton, a well-known patron (supporter) of the arts. "What I have done is yours," he wrote.

△ **Henry Wriothesley, Earl of Southampton,** was only 19 when Shakespeare dedicated his poems to him. The earl gave the poet £1,000 – a huge sum in those days.

◁ **A picture of London during a horrifying outbreak of the plague.** It was seen as God's way of punishing the sinful. Plague broke out regularly in the filthy city, where sewage and household waste of all kinds was simply thrown into the street or the River Thames. The heat of the summer helped the disease to spread, carried by fleas which lived on rats. Millions of these rats lived in the ageing timber-and-thatch houses of London. The plague was only curbed in the Great Fire of 1666, when many old buildings were destroyed.

◁ **Shakespeare rides out of London on his way to Stratford** to escape the dangers of the plague. He passes a cart carrying dead bodies to be buried. Some doors bear a red cross, to show that someone inside has the plague. The remains of a fire smoulder in the street. People believed, wrongly, that fires destroyed the germs in the air.

TO THE GLOBE

When the plague finally died down in the summer of 1594, the wandering troupes of actors began to gather again in London. New companies were formed, and new theatres were built and opened.

There were two main companies, which competed fiercely with each other. The Admiral's Men, led by the great actor Edward Alleyn and businessman Thomas Henslowe, were at first the most successful. Their rivals, the Lord Chamberlain's Men, were led by the bad-tempered James Burbage and his two sons. One thing would help them beat their rivals – a brilliant playwright.

Shakespeare was the ideal choice. He already had several popular plays to his name, and growing fame as a poet. He also had money to invest in the company. By the end of 1594, he was a sharer in the Lord Chamberlain's Men. He stayed with them for the rest of his career.

Over the next four years, Shakespeare wrote a further eight plays. Among them were some of his best-loved – the comedy *A Midsummer Night's Dream* and the tragic love story *Romeo and Juliet*. These were so popular that by 1598 the Lord Chamberlain's Men had become the leading company in London, and Shakespeare the most famous playwright.

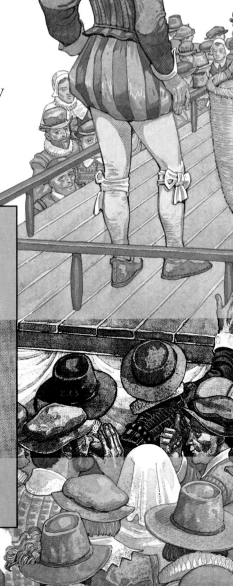

▷ **A scene from the comedy *The Merry Wives of Windsor***, which featured the fat and boastful Sir John Falstaff (centre). He had first appeared in *Henry IV*, and Queen Elizabeth had liked him so much that she asked for another play about him.

▷ **Richard Tarlton** was the most popular comic actor and clown of the late-Elizabethan period. He became one of Queen Elizabeth's private jesters. Although it is unlikely that he acted with Shakespeare, the playwright may have used him as the model for Yorick, the dead jester in *Hamlet*. Hamlet looks at Yorick's skull and remembers him as "a fellow of infinite jest, of most excellent fancy".

The most excellent Historie of the Merchant of VENICE.

With the extreame crueltie of *Shylocke* the Iewe towards the said Merchant, in cutting a just pound of his flesh: and the obtaining of P O R T I A by the choice of three Chests.

As it hath beene divers times acted by the *Lord Chamberlaine his Servants.*

Written by WILLIAM SHAKESPEARE.

LONDON,
M. P. for *Laurence Hayes*, and are to be sold his Shop on Fleetbridge 1637.

◁ **The title page of *The Merchant of Venice***, which was first performed in about 1597. The play portrays greed, and features one of Shakespeare's most famous characters, Shylock, a Jew. Shakespeare treats his character fairly, and in a famous speech Shylock shows how all people are the same: "If you prick us, do we not bleed? If you tickle us, do we not laugh?"

At first, the Lord Chamberlain's Men performed at The Theatre in Shoreditch. But in 1599 they moved to the new Globe Theatre. *As You Like It* and *Henry V* were among the first plays Shakespeare wrote for the company's new home. He had invested money in The Globe, and became one of its joint owners. He was now rich, and had already bought a big house in Stratford, called New Place, as a family home.

△ **New Place** in Stratford-upon-Avon, which Shakespeare bought in 1597 for £60. Anne and the children probably lived here while he was in London.

THE KING'S MEN

Shakespeare's plays drew huge audiences to The Globe. The company was so popular that it performed for the queen every Christmas. But in 1603 Elizabeth I died. She was succeeded by James I, who soon became the company's new patron.

Now, Shakespeare, Burbage and their colleagues were officially 'The King's Men'. They were paid £20 for a performance, and could wear a special scarlet costume on state occasions. They rode with the king when he made his grand entry into London in 1604.

Shakespeare worked harder than ever to produce new plays for the company, and went home to Stratford to write in peace. During this period, he wrote eleven plays, including some of his greatest – the tragedies *Hamlet*, *Othello*, *King Lear* and *Macbeth*. These grim tales showed how easily powerful men can be destroyed by weakness and ambition. However, Shakespeare took care that such themes did not anger the king.

▷ **The King's Men** perform *Hamlet* before James I at court. In this scene, Hamlet (right) meets the ghost of his father (left), murdered by his uncle. The ghost urges Hamlet to take revenge. Shakespeare often played the part of Hamlet's father.

△ **The commission, or licence, which James I granted to the Lord Chamberlain's Men in 1604.** It names several leading members of the company, and allows them "freely to use and exercise the Art and Faculty of playing Comedies, Tragedies, Histories". Within the next year, the company performed eleven plays at court – seven of them by Shakespeare.

▷ **A portrait of the new king, James I, painted by John de Gitz.** The king took a keen interest in drama, and wrote a letter of praise to Shakespeare in his own hand – a great compliment. But James was lazy and arrogant, and was soon very unpopular. In 1605, he and his parliament were nearly blown up by Catholic rebels in the Gunpowder Plot.

△ **Nathan Field** was an actor and playwright working in London at the same time as Shakespeare. He became a member of The King's Men in about 1616, possibly as a replacement for Shakespeare.

△ **A list of some of the performances given at court by 'His Majesty's Players'.** The plays by 'Shaxberd' included *Henry V* and *The Merchant of Venice*.

Shakespeare was not thought to have been an outstanding actor, but he knew a lot about acting skills, and wrote lines and directions which suited the actors in the company. This is one reason why his plays were so successful.

In *Hamlet*, he described the arrival at court of a group of travelling players. The scene shows how well he understood the actor's life. Hamlet insists that the actors should be properly looked after: "Let them be well used, for they are the abstract and brief chroniclers of the time." Then he expertly tells the players how to speak their lines: "Suit the action to the word, the word to the action."

In 1608, the company was in such a strong position that it took over a second theatre. This was the Blackfriars Theatre across the Thames. It was smaller, but much more comfortable and elegant than the draughty Globe, with a roof, heating and lighting. Now plays could be put on all through the year.

THE LAST PLAYS

By 1608, Shakespeare was in his mid forties. This, for the time, was nearly old age, because people had shorter lives then. His son, Hamnet, had died young, at only 11 years old, in 1596. Shakespeare was already a grandfather (Susanna had a baby that year), and in 1609 his mother died.

△ **Sir Francis Bacon (1561-1626)**, above right, was a writer and politician who helped to advance scientific knowledge. In the 19th century, some people thought that Bacon was the author of the plays we think of as Shakespeare's.

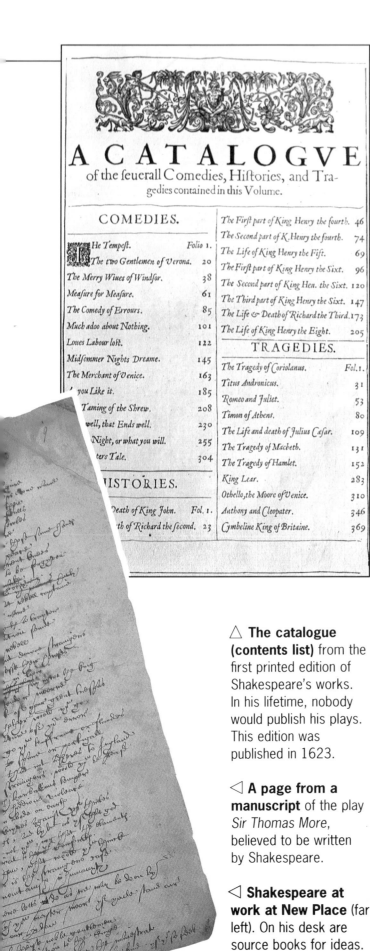

A CATALOGVE
of the seuerall Comedies, Histories, and Tragedies contained in this Volume.

△ **The catalogue (contents list)** from the first printed edition of Shakespeare's works. In his lifetime, nobody would publish his plays. This edition was published in 1623.

◁ **A page from a manuscript** of the play *Sir Thomas More*, believed to be written by Shakespeare.

◁ **Shakespeare at work at New Place** (far left). On his desk are source books for ideas. He is holding a quill pen.

▷ **A printer's workshop** in about 1630. Printing had begun in England in 1476, and had quickly developed into an important trade. By Shakespeare's time, printed books were common, and more people could read than ever before.

Now that they had the second theatre at Blackfriars, The King's Men needed even more new plays. They took on three more playwrights: Ben Jonson, Francis Beaumont and John Fletcher.

Shakespeare must have encouraged the new men, but in return they inspired him to attempt a new style of drama – the 'romances' *Cymbeline*, *The Tempest* and *The Winter's Tale*. Half-way between tragedy and comedy, these plays contain strange scenes and characters. *The Tempest*, for example, is set on an island which is "full of noises, sounds and sweet airs, that give delight, and hurt not".

Shakespeare and Fletcher also wrote plays together, including *Henry VIII* and *The Two Noble Kinsmen*. Fletcher probably wrote most of the text, with Shakespeare working on the grand speeches. Another play, *Cardenio*, unfortunately has not survived.

In 1609, a London publisher issued a collection called *Shakespeare's Sonnets*. It contained over 150 poems, each in the strict 14-line form of the sonnet. Many were about death and ageing; others were love poems, addressed to an unknown woman with black hair: "Shall I compare thee to a summer's day? Thou art more lovely and more temperate".

BACK TO STRATFORD

By now, the two theatres were running smoothly, and were packed every night. The King's Men were growing rich, and there were new writers to supply plays. At last, Shakespeare had time to rest. After about 1612, he seems to have written nothing new. He now spent most of his time in Stratford.

△ **Shakespeare's sonnets** pose many questions about his later life. The collection was dedicated to a Mr W.H., "the onlie begetter of these insuing sonnets". Was this Henry Wriothesley? And who is the young man who is mentioned in the earlier sonnets as 'sweet boy' and 'my lovely boy'? Perhaps it was the son of another patron?

▽ **William and Anne Shakespeare in the gardens of New Place.** The house no longer stands, having been pulled down in 1759.

△ **"A praty house of brike and tymber,"** was how Shakespeare referred to New Place. Behind the house, on the left, is Stratford Guild Chapel which still stands today.

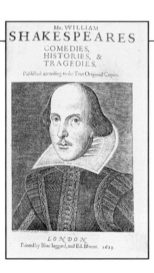

▷ **The portrait of Shakespeare by Martin Droeshout** in the 1623 *First Folio*, the first edition of his collected plays. It was said by Ben Jonson to be a good likeness. Jonson also wrote that Shakespeare was "not of an Age, but for all time".

▷ **The sculpture of Shakespeare's monument in Stratford.** Although it makes the poet look dull and plump, it is thought to look much like him. The inscription underneath ends: "Curst be he that moves my bones".

Shakespeare was a wealthy man. He owned land and houses in Stratford, and in 1613 he bought a large house in Blackfriars and rented it to a tenant. He was a famous and respected citizen of his native town, living with his family among friends he had known since childhood. His theatrical friends from London, including Ben Jonson, also visited him.

▽ **The last page of Shakespeare's will**, with his signature, made a month before his death. The signature is very shaky. It may have been the last time he picked up a pen.

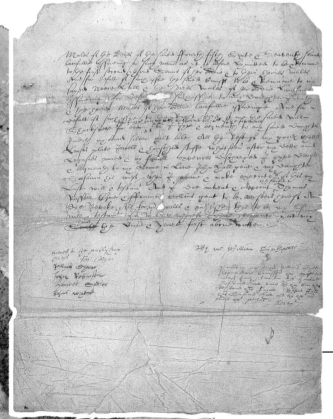

Now that he was no longer writing, Shakespeare turned his energy and talent towards his garden. The grounds of New Place were carefully laid out with orchards, trees and vines. His plays show that he had a great love of plants and gardening. In *Henry IV*, *Part 2*, fat John Falstaff is welcomed by a country friend: "You shall see mine orchard, where, in an arbour, we will eat a last year's pippin [apple] of my own grafting, with a dish of caraways".

But there was also sadness. By 1613, six of Shakespeare's seven brothers and sisters were dead, and he began to prepare carefully for his own death. Early in 1616 he made his will. As he had no male heir, he left his land and property to his eldest daughter, Susanna. Judith, his other daughter, received £150. The only mention of his wife Anne was that she should receive "my second-best bed". But she would get more. By law, Anne would inherit one third of her husband's estate. Shakespeare also left £10 to the poor people of Stratford.

By now, he was probably a sick man. He died on 23 April 1616 – aged 52 – and was buried inside Holy Trinity Church. In 1623, a monument was placed there in his memory.

THE LEGACY OF SHAKESPEARE

Shakespeare's plays remained very popular for some years after his death. They were exciting, and could be easily understood by ordinary people. But by about 1660, they began to fall out of fashion. The new theatres were grand and ornate, with elaborate scenery. They did not suit Shakespeare's work.

▽ **Thousands of people come every year to explore Stratford-upon-Avon** and watch performances of Shakespeare's plays here at the Royal Shakespeare Theatre.

In the early 1700s, Shakespeare's plays were often criticized for being rude and gloomy. Some playwrights tried to improve them. But his reputation slowly grew again. By the early 1800s, he was seen as the greatest of English writers. His understanding of how people get on with, argue or fight one another over money, land, property or power was unequalled by any other writer. He wrote brilliantly, even of everyday things like food, the weather and animals. And Shakespeare's writings show that people's ideas, attitudes and wishes are the same today as they were in Tudor times. Nowadays, his plays are regularly performed, made into films and even stored on CD-ROMs.

▷ **A puppeteer in Madras, India**, puts on a Shakespeare play in the street for young children. Shakespeare's works are performed in many different ways.

▷ **The George Inn** at Southwark (far right). In Shakespeare's time, travelling players would perform in the courtyard, watched by people in the galleries.

GLOSSARY

bailiff leading official of a town, usually elected for a year.

church register books in which baptisms, marriages and funeral services for the parish are recorded.

comedy play or other work which tells a humorous story and has a happy ending.

dedicate to write a book or perform a play in honour of someone.

folio large size of book, whose pages are a standard sheet of paper folded in half.

jester clown or fool, usually employed by a monarch.

licence document giving official permission for a specific activity.

manuscript a book written by hand.

pageant colourful scene from a story, presented as a procession or display.

patron someone who supports, pays or protects people.

playwright writer of plays.

quill pen pen made from the sharpened feather of a bird – usually a goose.

season set period in which a certain number of performances are given.

source book chronicles of history, stories and other books used by a writer for ideas and details.

text the words of something written or printed.

tragedy serious play in which the central character is ruined or destroyed.

troupe company or group of touring actors, dancers or singers.

will the written wishes of a person about sharing his or her property among people after he or she dies.

▷ **Stratford-upon-Avon**, showing the major places related to Shakespeare's life and plays.

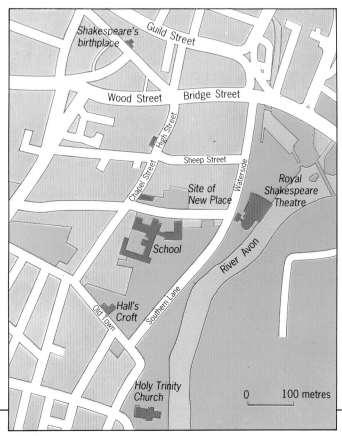

TIMECHART of Shakespeare's plays

(The dates are approximate)

1589-91 Henry VI, Parts 1, 2 and 3
Titus Andronicus

1593 Richard III
Venus and Adonis
The Comedy of Errors
The Taming of the Shrew

1594 Two Gentlemen of Verona
Love's Labour's Lost
Romeo and Juliet

1595 Richard II
A Midsummer Night's Dream

1596 King John
The Merchant of Venice

1597 Henry IV, Parts 1 and 2

1598 Much Ado About Nothing
The Merry Wives of Windsor

1599 Julius Caesar
As You Like It
Henry V

1600 Twelfth Night

1601 Troilus and Cressida
Hamlet

1602 All's Well That Ends Well

1603 Othello
Measure For Measure

1604 Timon of Athens

1605 King Lear

1606 Macbeth

1607 Coriolanus

1608 Antony and Cleopatra
Pericles

1609 Cymbeline

1610 The Winter's Tale
The Tempest

1613 Henry VIII
The Two Noble Kinsmen

INDEX